The Customer Train

The Customer Train

JC Quintana

CONTENTS

To those who believe in the power of genuine connection,
This book is for you—the leaders, visionaries, and everyday heroes who understand that business is more than numbers and transactions. It's about people. It's about the trust you build, the moments you share, and the relationships that grow when you put customers at the heart of your organization.

May this story inspire you to keep building those bridges, nurturing those connections, and reminding the world that the most meaningful journeys are the ones where we travel together.

Thank you for your commitment to making every interaction, every experience, and every journey matter.

With gratitude,

JC Quintana

Part 1: The Building of the Tracks

Chapter I: Departure from the Station

The day was bright and alive with the hum of anticipation as the customer train, a marvel of modern engineering and collaboration, prepared for its first departure. Crowds gathered at stations across the world—Tokyo, Sydney, Dubai, London, and Chicago—each station a unique blend of culture and technology, all interconnected through a web of steel tracks stretching across continents. Passengers of all walks of life, dressed in vibrant colors and carrying stories of their own, filled the platforms. Some boarded the train with eagerness, others with quiet hope, and a few with a sense of uncertainty. But they all shared the same destination: forward.

The train itself, a gleaming colossus, represented more than just transportation. It was the manifestation of a dream that had been years in the making, a testament to the vision of the architects who designed the sprawling network. They believed that commerce, like the train, should move people and ideas swiftly, but also meaningfully. It wasn't just about speed; it was about creating a connection, bridging gaps, and uniting communities.

The architects, inspired by their predecessors, had taken their time to build this network. They sought the best engineers and conductors from all corners of the globe—people with the knowledge to navigate complex routes but also with the compassion to understand that passengers were not just numbers; they were individuals with their own destinations, hopes, and dreams. These engineers and conductors were chosen not only for their technical prowess but for their humanity. They knew that the customer train was more than just a machine; it was an experience.

As the departure hour approached, the platform came alive with the sound of conversations, laughter, and the hiss of steam escaping from the locomotive. The head engineer, a seasoned veteran named **Gregor**, stood at the helm, his eyes scanning the crowd. He knew the responsibility that came with his position. The train's success depended not only on his ability to guide it along its tracks but also on his understanding of the ever-changing landscapes it would cross.

Beside him, **Eloise**, the head conductor, moved through the crowds, speaking with passengers, answering questions, and ensuring everyone felt welcomed. She believed that her role went beyond checking tickets; she was the bridge between the train's operation and the passengers' experience. Her calm voice and attentive demeanor put travelers at ease, and she made it a point to learn the names of the regulars, to understand their stories.

With a final call of "All aboard!" from Eloise, the doors of the customer train closed, and the massive wheels began to turn. The train lurched forward, pulling away from the station and embarking on its journey. As it glided along the tracks, passengers looked out of the windows, some seeing familiar sights, while others saw new landscapes unfold before them. For many, this was more than just a trip; it was a chance to explore, to reach places they had only dreamed of, and to connect with others on the way.

Inside the train, the carriages were designed to accommodate the varying needs of its passengers. There were quiet compartments for those seeking solitude and reflection, lively dining cars where passengers could share meals and stories, and comfortable lounges for those who wished to network and collaborate during the journey. The architects had thought of everything, ensuring that the train would not only take its passengers to their destinations but also provide them with the space and environment to enjoy the journey.

As the train picked up speed, Gregor adjusted the controls, feeling the power of the engine beneath his hands. He knew that guiding the train wasn't just about the mechanics; it was about anticipating changes in weather, adjusting to the terrain, and ensuring that the train remained on schedule. It required constant attention, foresight, and an understanding of the rhythm of the tracks. Eloise joined him in the engine room, her eyes alight with the same passion she had felt on her first day as a conductor. "This is it," she said, her voice filled with excitement. "The journey begins."

Gregor nodded, glancing over at her. "Let's make it count. Every passenger, every station, every stop matters."

The architects watched from their headquarters as the train disappeared into the horizon, their hearts filled with hope and pride. They had built something magnificent—a system that, if nurtured and maintained with care, could change lives. They knew there would be challenges, that the tracks ahead were not always smooth, and that there would be times when the train faced delays or difficulties. But they had faith in the engineers, the conductors, and, most importantly, the passengers themselves.

The architects had ensured that each person had a voice, a chance to shape their journey. They understood that the train's true power lay not in its speed or its efficiency but in its ability to connect people, to take them to where they truly needed to be.

As the train powered forward, crossing bridges and racing through tunnels, the sun set, casting a warm glow over the tracks. The night came alive with the lights of distant cities, and the train continued on its way, carrying the hopes and dreams of all who traveled on it. The journey had only just begun, and the tracks stretched out, promising new adventures, connections, and destinations.

And so, the customer train set off, not just a machine of commerce but a vessel of purpose, a symbol of what was possible when people, technology, and vision aligned.

Chapter II: The Engineers and the Architects

The success of the customer train was not merely the product of its powerful engines or its intricate network of tracks. It was a result of the people behind it—those who believed that the train was more than a vehicle; it was a promise. The architects who designed the system knew that to fulfill this promise, they needed the right people at the helm—individuals who were not only experts in their field but who also understood the human element behind every journey.

The architects, a diverse group of visionaries from different corners of the globe, gathered for their annual summit in the grand hall of **Central Station**. The room, filled with blueprints and models of trains, bustled with energy. Engineers, conductors, and station masters exchanged ideas, building a collective vision for the future of the railway. At the head of the room stood **Valen**, a young architect whose family lineage tied directly back to the founding builders of the railway. He held a position of great responsibility, as well as a deep sense of duty to uphold the legacy left by those who had come before him.

Valen cleared his throat, and the room quieted. "We have come a long way since the first track was laid," he began. "Our trains cross continents and connect people from every walk of life. But to continue this journey, we must remain committed to our principles. It is not enough to build tracks and engines—we must build relationships."

Around the room, heads nodded in agreement. The architects understood that the success of their enterprise was rooted in the trust they had built with their passengers. They knew that the customer train had to be more than just efficient; it had to be an experience that made people feel valued. This required more than technological advancement—it required leadership that inspired collaboration and fostered a sense of shared purpose.

Gregor, the head engineer from Chapter I, stood up. His hands, calloused from years of work on the tracks, showed his dedication. "We need engineers who not only understand the mechanics of the train but also the needs of our passengers. It's not enough to know how to operate the engines; we must anticipate the challenges that lie ahead—weather, terrain, and even the seasons. But above all, we need engineers who understand that every decision they make impacts the lives of our passengers."

Valen smiled, appreciating Gregor's insight. "Exactly, Gregor. But it's not just the engineers who must be prepared. Our conductors—those who interact with our passengers daily—must be equipped with the skills to communicate effectively and with empathy. We need them to be the bridge between the technology and the people who rely on it."

A hand rose from the back of the room, belonging to **Amara**, one of the most respected conductors in the network. Her experience had earned her the trust of passengers and her colleagues alike. "We have the technology to make the trains faster, but speed isn't everything. We need to remember that passengers aren't just looking for the quickest route; they're looking for a journey that feels meaningful. That's where we, as conductors, come in. We have the power to make every journey memorable by listening to their needs and adapting."

The architects turned to listen as Amara continued. "I've seen the impact of a smile, of taking the time to help a passenger find their seat or answering their questions with patience. These small gestures matter. We need conductors who understand that they aren't just managing tickets; they are the heart of this operation."

The architects exchanged thoughtful glances, and Valen felt a surge of pride. He knew that the architects' vision was in good hands. "Well said, Amara. Conductors are indeed the heart, and engineers the backbone. But even beyond that, our entire system relies on an unseen force—the station masters, the porters, the maintenance teams, and everyone who keeps the customer train moving."

He paused, gesturing to the walls around them where the **Customer Railway Blueprint** was displayed. "The nine precepts we developed years ago remain our guiding principles. These foundations have kept us aligned with our purpose. We must remind ourselves that the train's strength is not just in its speed or efficiency, but in the sum of all these parts working together."

Valen then directed everyone's attention to a large map of the network. "Our tracks stretch far and wide, and while some routes are traveled by thousands, others lead to remote and unique destinations. We must ensure that we're building tracks that matter—tracks that take people where they need to go, even if only a few passengers need that route. It's not about filling every train to capacity; it's about making sure that every passenger feels they're on the right path."

The room buzzed with renewed energy. The architects and engineers debated the best routes to lay and the technology needed to maintain the tracks. But in every conversation, the focus remained on the passengers—those who depended on the customer train not just to reach their destinations but to feel connected along the way.

Valen concluded the summit with a final address. "We will continue to build and innovate, but let us never forget our mission: to make every journey purposeful, every passenger valued, and every connection meaningful. The tracks we lay today are the paths our future will follow."

As the summit came to a close, the architects, engineers, and conductors left with a sense of unity. They understood that the true power of the customer train lay in its ability to bring people together, to serve them not just as passengers but as partners in a shared journey. The success of the network depended on more than the mechanics of steel and steam; it depended on the people who believed in the journey itself.

And so, the architects set forth with a renewed sense of purpose, ready to lay tracks that would lead to destinations both familiar and new. The future of the customer train was bright, and they knew that as long as they stayed true to their principles, every journey would matter.

Chapter III: The Customer Railway Blueprint

The architects knew that building a customer train network wasn't merely about laying tracks and constructing stations; it was about designing a system that could grow, adapt, and serve people for generations. At the heart of their vision was the **Customer Railway Blueprint**—a set of nine precepts that would guide the railway's expansion and ensure its long-term success. This blueprint, crafted with care and foresight, was not just a technical document; it was a philosophy, a commitment to the passengers and communities the customer train would touch.

Gathered once again in the central hall of **Station One**, the original architects stood before the blueprint displayed across a massive screen. Valen, the young architect whose family legacy was tied to the railway's founding, took the stage to present the guiding principles.

"Before we discuss the specifics of our routes, stations, and engines, we must remind ourselves of the foundations that will support everything we build," he began. "These precepts will not only guide our operations but will also remind us of the core reason why we do what we do: to connect people meaningfully."

The architects and engineers watched intently as Valen revealed the blueprint's nine precepts:

1. **Trains Need Tracks to Meaningful Destinations**

   "Passengers aren't all heading to the same place," Valen explained. "Some will board our trains to reach bustling cities, while others will seek remote destinations. It's our responsibility to build tracks that serve these diverse needs, ensuring every route is purposeful and aligned with where people need and want to go."

2. **Focus on Getting People to Their Destinations, Not Just Moving Trains**

   The architects nodded in agreement. "We must avoid the temptation of simply filling trains and maximizing speed," Valen continued. "The value of our service lies in taking the right passengers to the right destinations, creating journeys that feel tailored and intentional."

3. **Communicate Before Passengers Miss the Train**

   "It's not enough for passengers to hear the horn; they need to know when and where to board well in advance," Valen stressed. "Our stations must be accessible, and our communication must be clear. We must meet passengers where they are, ensuring they have all the information they need to embark on their journey."

4. **Announcing 'All Aboard' Is Just the Beginning**

   Valen gestured to the conductors in the room. "The departure call is a signal that everything is ready, but it's also a reminder that our work doesn't stop once passengers are on board. From ensuring the train runs on time to making every passenger feel welcome, our responsibilities extend beyond the station."

5. **Trains Depend on Many Hands Working Together**

   The screen displayed images of station masters, porters, engineers, and maintenance teams. "The success of our train network relies on the collaborative efforts of countless individuals," Valen said. "We must recognize and value every person's contribution. Without their dedication, no train reaches its destination safely."

6. **Build Trust Through Consistency and Reliability**

   "Passengers must know that when they board our trains, they can count on us to deliver them safely and on time," Valen emphasized. "Trust is earned through consistent performance and reliability, and it's the cornerstone of our relationship with those who choose to travel with us."

7. **Listen More Than You Speak**

   "If we want to serve our passengers well, we must first listen to them," Valen reminded the audience. "Our stations should be places where passengers feel comfortable sharing their experiences. Feedback isn't just valuable; it's essential for our growth and improvement."

8. **Empower the People Who Serve the Passengers**

   "Our conductors and engineers are on the front lines," Valen continued. "They are the face of our network, and their ability to make decisions and connect with passengers is crucial. We must give them the tools, training, and autonomy they need to lead with confidence and care."

9. **Evolve Without Losing Sight of the Journey**

Valen's tone grew solemn. "Innovation is necessary, and technology can help us move faster and serve more passengers. But we must never lose sight of the fact that the journey itself is as important as the destination. If we focus solely on progress, we risk forgetting why the customer train was built in the first place."

As Valen finished, the room fell into a contemplative silence. These precepts, displayed prominently on the screen, were the heart of the Customer Railway Blueprint. They encapsulated the vision of the architects: a railway that was not just a network of tracks but a system built on trust, service, and connection.

Elias, one of the engineers who had attended the previous summit, rose to speak. "These precepts remind us that our job goes beyond building and operating machines. It's about ensuring that the technology we create supports these principles. We can't afford to automate away the human element; instead, we must integrate technology in ways that enhance, not diminish, the passenger experience."

Amara, the head conductor, nodded in agreement. "Our role as conductors is more than operational—it's relational. We need to understand our passengers, communicate with them, and be present for their needs. If we align our actions with these precepts, we can create an experience that people trust and cherish."

The architects spent the rest of the day working in teams, applying the blueprint's precepts to the various challenges and opportunities facing the railway. They discussed how to modernize the stations while maintaining their accessibility, how to use data to improve route efficiency without compromising passenger comfort, and how to train the next generation of engineers and conductors to carry forward the principles established by the original founders.

By the end of the day, the architects had not only reaffirmed their commitment to the blueprint but had also developed actionable plans to bring their vision to life. They knew that the road ahead would not be without its challenges. Balancing speed, efficiency, and customer experience required constant vigilance and adaptability. But they also knew that as long as they stayed true to the precepts, they could create a railway system that was not only efficient but also human-centric.

Before the summit ended, Valen made one final announcement. "We will inscribe these precepts on the walls of every station and into the engines of every train. They will be more than words; they will be our promise to every passenger, engineer, and conductor who becomes a part of this journey."

As the architects dispersed, they carried with them the weight of responsibility but also the excitement of what lay ahead. The blueprint wasn't just a set of rules; it was the roadmap for a thriving, evolving network that would continue to connect people in meaningful ways for generations.

And so, the tracks stretched out before them, ready to be built, not just to move passengers from one place to another but to guide them on a journey that mattered.

Part 2: The Derailment

Chapter IV: The Era of Prosperity

In the years following the implementation of the Customer Railway Blueprint, the customer train network experienced unprecedented growth and prosperity. The principles set forth by the architects guided every decision, every track laid, and every route chosen. Across continents, stations bustled with activity, and passengers spoke of the customer train with admiration. The system thrived as engineers and conductors embodied the values of trust, connection, and service that had been inscribed in the blueprint.

At the heart of this golden era was a sense of collaboration and shared vision. The original architects, led by Valen, remained active, mentoring the new generation of engineers and conductors. They worked alongside visionaries like Gregor, who designed engines that maximized both speed and comfort, and Amara, who became a champion of passenger experience, ensuring that every journey was as fulfilling as the destination itself.

The train stations were alive with the energy of progress. In cities like Dubai and Tokyo, travelers mingled with business leaders, artists, and explorers, exchanging ideas and stories. The customer train was no longer just a means of transportation; it was a network that fostered community and opportunity. People from all walks of life boarded the trains, knowing that they were not simply moving from point A to point B but becoming part of a larger, shared experience.

New architects emerged, inspired by the legacy of their predecessors. They built smaller, more agile customer trains that could reach destinations off the main routes. These trains were designed to serve remote communities, bringing commerce and opportunity to regions that had once been difficult to access. These architects believed in decentralization, giving the smaller stations autonomy to create routes that suited their unique needs. This innovation was celebrated as a testament to the flexibility and adaptability of the customer railway.

The prosperity brought with it a new wave of technological advancements. **Suri**, a young technology specialist, introduced an automation system that optimized train schedules, monitored track conditions in real-time, and even streamlined passenger communication through an advanced app. This technology allowed the engineers and conductors to focus more on human interaction, while the automated systems handled the technical details. Passengers received updates directly on their devices, ensuring that they were informed of every aspect of their journey.

The architects' vision of a balanced, technology-enhanced, and customer-focused railway seemed to be realized. Valen and his team celebrated the progress, confident that the customer train had reached a new pinnacle. The news was filled with stories of the customer train's impact on communities: increased access to education, commerce, and cultural exchange. The network was heralded as an example of how technology and humanity could coexist harmoniously.

However, as the network expanded and profits soared, new voices began to emerge within the ranks of the architects and engineers—voices that focused less on the passenger experience and more on maximizing efficiency and profitability. Some of the new architects saw the potential for even greater profit margins and argued that the customer train could become even faster and more streamlined if they adjusted the principles slightly. Their argument was compelling: with the right technology, they could transport more passengers in less time, leading to increased revenue and reduced operational costs.

At first, these suggestions were met with resistance. Valen and the older generation of architects insisted that the focus remain on passengers and their experiences. "Our success has always come from balancing speed with connection, efficiency with empathy," Valen reminded the assembly during one of their annual summits. "Remember that the train is not just a machine; it's a promise to our passengers."

But as profits continued to climb and the demand for faster travel increased, the allure of greater efficiency became hard to ignore. The new generation of architects, influenced by the successes of their agile, smaller trains, began to believe that they could apply the same principles to the larger network. Why not optimize everything for speed, they argued, if the technology allowed it?

Aiden, one of the rising architects and a vocal proponent of increased efficiency, became a key figure in this shift. "The world is moving faster, and we must adapt. Passengers want to reach their destinations quickly, and we have the means to provide that," he insisted. His ideas found support among some of the younger engineers who had grown up during the golden age of prosperity but had not experienced the struggles of building the network from scratch. They believed that the success of the customer train meant it was time to take risks, to push the limits of what was possible.

Valen watched these developments with caution. He had seen the dangers of overconfidence before and knew that losing sight of the original mission could lead to unforeseen consequences. However, the pressure from within the organization and the external demand for faster services became too great. Reluctantly, he agreed to allow Aiden and his team to experiment with new routes and systems designed to maximize speed and capacity.

The new changes brought immediate results. Passenger numbers surged as the trains became faster and schedules more frequent. Efficiency reached an all-time high, and profits soared. Aiden's automated scheduling system minimized delays, and Suri's technology ensured that every train ran at peak performance. The media hailed the architects as visionaries of a new era, and even Valen, despite his reservations, felt the excitement of their success.

But beneath the surface, cracks were beginning to show. The focus on speed and efficiency had led to a subtle shift in priorities. Engineers were now tasked with maximizing output rather than ensuring the comfort and satisfaction of passengers. Conductors were given strict quotas to meet, which meant spending less time interacting with passengers and more time managing schedules and processes. The app that had once been a tool for convenience became a mechanism for micromanaging every aspect of the passenger journey, leaving less room for the personal touch that had defined the customer train's experience.

Amara, who had been an advocate for the passenger experience, began to notice the difference. "The passengers used to feel like partners in the journey," she observed to Valen during one of their check-in meetings. "Now, they're starting to feel like commodities."

Valen felt the truth in her words but found himself caught in a difficult position. The success of the customer train had become so tied to its efficiency and speed that any deviation from the current path felt like a risk he wasn't sure they could afford to take. "We'll monitor the situation," he told Amara. "But for now, the system is working. We need to give it time."

Despite the warning signs, the customer train continued its journey through an era of prosperity, faster and more efficient than ever before. The architects and engineers celebrated their achievements, convinced that they had reached the pinnacle of success. But as the wheels of the customer train turned faster, the focus on the journey itself began to blur, setting the stage for the derailment that would follow.

Chapter V: The Shift Toward Speed

As the demand for faster service grew, the customer train network found itself at a crossroads. The architects, who once championed balance and human connection, faced pressure from all directions—passengers seeking shorter travel times, investors looking for higher profits, and a new generation of engineers eager to showcase the potential of their advanced technology. The allure of speed became the dominant force guiding the network's expansion, overshadowing the foundational principles that had once defined the customer railway.

Aiden, now the lead architect of the efficiency movement, proposed a series of sweeping changes. "If we want to stay competitive, we need to shift our focus entirely," he insisted during one of the architect summits. "The world is moving at an unprecedented pace, and we need to adapt. We have the technology to double our train speeds, automate our systems further, and cut down travel times. The time has come to put our capabilities to the test."

His proposals were met with mixed reactions. Some of the younger architects and engineers, who had joined the network during the prosperous years, cheered Aiden's vision. They saw this as a chance to prove themselves, to push the boundaries of what the customer train could accomplish. They believed that faster trains would mean more passengers and, consequently, more revenue. But others, particularly those who had helped build the network from its early days, watched with growing unease.

Valen, still respected as a voice of reason among the architects, voiced his concerns. "Increasing speed is tempting, but we must be cautious," he warned. "Our blueprint emphasizes balance. Efficiency should never come at the expense of the passenger experience. If we move too quickly, we risk losing sight of why the customer train was created in the first place."

But Aiden, emboldened by his growing influence and the success of his past projects, pressed forward. He had already implemented pilot programs that showed promising results—shorter travel times and increased ticket sales. He knew that as long as he delivered numbers, the network's leadership and investors would support his vision. "We've spent years prioritizing experience," he replied to Valen. "Now, it's time to prioritize performance."

The shift began gradually. First, Aiden's team introduced new, streamlined scheduling systems that reduced station wait times to a bare minimum. Then, Suri's technology was further integrated, automating everything from track monitoring to passenger communication. The once-bustling stations, where conductors and passengers had shared stories and advice, were transformed into efficient hubs where interactions were reduced to quick exchanges of information.

Conductors, who had once been the heart of the customer train experience, were now tasked with adhering strictly to efficiency quotas. They no longer had the time to engage with passengers personally; instead, they were monitored closely, ensuring that every action aligned with the new speed-centered protocols. Eloise, a veteran conductor known for her dedication, felt the impact of these changes keenly. "We're no longer conductors; we're operators," she confided to Amara during a rare moment of pause. "I used to know our passengers by name, but now, I barely have time to look up from my schedule."

Amara, having already voiced her concerns to Valen, could see the shift affecting morale across the network. Engineers who had once taken pride in ensuring passenger comfort were now focused solely on performance metrics. The emphasis on speed meant that maintenance teams worked under immense pressure, with less time to inspect and repair tracks. "It's not just about the passengers," she said. "Even our own people are starting to feel like cogs in a machine."

But despite these concerns, the new system produced results. The trains became faster, and efficiency soared. Passenger numbers increased as people sought quicker ways to travel, and the profits followed. The media hailed the transformation as the dawn of a new era for the customer train, praising the architects for their vision and innovation. Aiden, in particular, was celebrated as the mastermind behind the network's evolution, his face appearing on magazine covers as a symbol of modern leadership.

Valen, torn between his loyalty to the architects and his growing doubts, watched as the customer train seemed to accelerate away from the principles he had helped establish. He knew that the network had to evolve to stay relevant, but he struggled with the speed and direction of the change. "I fear we are becoming a machine without a soul," he confided to Gregor, the head engineer. "We've gained speed, but at what cost?"

Gregor nodded solemnly. "The engines run faster than ever, but I've noticed the cracks forming. We're pushing the limits of our technology, and we're not giving our people the time they need to maintain the tracks properly. It's only a matter of time before something goes wrong."

The cracks were not only metaphorical. As the focus shifted entirely to speed, the tracks themselves began to show signs of strain. Engineers working under pressure overlooked small issues that, over time, compounded into larger problems. Maintenance teams, spread thin by the demands of the new schedules, struggled to keep up. Stations that once bustled with life became rushed environments where passengers felt the cold efficiency of the system but missed the warmth that had once defined their journeys.

Passengers, too, began to notice the change. Some appreciated the quicker travel times, but many felt a growing sense of detachment. They boarded and disembarked with little interaction, guided only by automated announcements and digital displays. The train, which had once been a place of connection, started to feel impersonal. Regular passengers who had once been greeted by name found themselves lost in the efficiency of the new system.

Among these passengers was **Lian**, a young commuter who had grown up listening to her grandfather's stories of the golden age of the customer train. As she watched the changes unfold, she felt a disconnect between the tales of community and connection her grandfather had cherished and the reality she now experienced. "The customer train used to feel like home," she mused to herself, "but now it's just a way to get somewhere."

The architects, still basking in the glow of their success, overlooked these signals. They continued to push for greater speed, believing that as long as the trains moved faster and profits grew, they were on the right track. But the warning signs were becoming impossible to ignore. Delays, once rare, became more frequent as the strained tracks required more frequent repairs. Passengers who had once been loyal began to voice their frustrations, citing the impersonal nature of the service and the stress of rushed schedules.

Aiden, focused on maintaining his image and continuing the network's rapid expansion, brushed off these complaints. "Change is never easy," he told his team. "People will adjust. We are giving them what they need: speed."

But as the trains continued to race down the tracks, the system that had once been built on balance and collaboration grew increasingly unstable. The architects and engineers, once celebrated for their ability to connect people, now found themselves caught in a cycle of chasing numbers, losing sight of the passengers who had always been the heart of the journey.

The customer train, now hurtling forward at unprecedented speeds, was no longer a symbol of connection but a machine designed for output. And as the cracks in the tracks deepened, the question loomed: how long could they sustain this speed before everything came crashing down?

Chapter VI: The Tragic Derail

The customer train, once a symbol of connection and progress, had become something else entirely. The tracks, now pushed beyond their limits, strained under the weight of the ever-accelerating engines. Passengers, who had once felt at home aboard the train, now moved through stations that had lost their warmth and charm. Automated systems guided them through a maze of efficiency, but the human touch—the very soul of the customer train—had all but disappeared.

Aiden, the architect behind the shift toward speed, remained steadfast in his belief that the changes were necessary. Despite the growing number of complaints and the visible signs of stress on the system, he refused to slow down. "The future waits for no one," he declared in his well-known battle cry at a gathering of the network's leaders. "We must continue to innovate and push the boundaries, or we will be left behind."

Suri, whose technology had been instrumental in automating the system, watched with increasing concern. She had joined the customer train with a vision of using technology to enhance the passenger experience, not replace it. But as she saw more conductors sidelined and more passengers treated as data points rather than individuals, she wondered if they had gone too far. "We've built a powerful machine," she confided to Valen, "but it's losing sight of the people it was meant to serve."

Valen, who had tried to warn Aiden and the other architects about the risks of focusing solely on speed, now felt the weight of his hesitation. He had been torn between his duty to protect the legacy of the original architects and the pressure to modernize. But as reports of delays and infrastructure issues continued to mount, he knew they were on the brink of disaster. "We are riding on borrowed time," he said quietly, his voice heavy with regret.

The train stations, once vibrant centers of activity, began to show signs of neglect. The maintenance teams, overwhelmed by the demands of keeping the accelerated schedules, struggled to keep up. Tracks that had once been inspected with care now received only cursory checks, as engineers were pushed to focus on speed rather than safety. Cracks that would have been repaired in the past were left unattended, and small problems grew into significant hazards.

One evening, as the night shift engineers worked on a particularly strained section of the track outside the city of Prague, they noticed a warning light flashing on their diagnostics panel. It indicated a structural weakness in the track—one that could become catastrophic if not addressed immediately. But with schedules to maintain and no time allocated for a full inspection, they were forced to make a quick fix and move on, hoping it would hold until the next maintenance cycle.

Meanwhile, in the control center, Suri monitored the situation. She saw the warning signal and alerted the engineers, but with pressure mounting to keep the trains moving, her concerns were dismissed. "It's a minor issue," they told her. "The schedule must be maintained." Unease settled in her chest, but she felt powerless to stop what was unfolding.

As dawn broke, the customer train left the station in Prague, filled with passengers on their morning commute. Gregor, the head engineer, was at the controls, his eyes scanning the monitors. He had felt the growing strain within the system for months, and every day he feared they were pushing too close to the edge. His hands gripped the controls tightly as the train picked up speed, his gaze flickering to the instruments that tracked the condition of the tracks ahead.

At first, everything seemed normal. The train glided smoothly through the cityscape, its passengers engrossed in their routines. Some read the news on their devices, others chatted in hushed voices, and a few simply stared out the windows, watching the world rush by. The atmosphere was calm, almost serene—until a sudden jolt shook the train.

Passengers looked up, startled, as the train lurched again, this time with more force. Gregor's hands moved rapidly over the controls as warning lights flared across the panel. "There's instability in the track ahead," he called out to his team, his voice tense. "Brace for impact!"

But it was too late. The train, moving at its accelerated speed, hit the weakened section of track with a thunderous crash. The carriages shuddered violently, and the sound of metal scraping against metal filled the air as the train began to derail. Passengers screamed as the force threw them from their seats, luggage and belongings scattered in chaos. Windows shattered, and the train careened off the tracks, sliding to a halt in a cloud of smoke and dust.

Amara, who had been on duty that morning, moved quickly through the train, helping passengers find safety exits. Her years of experience and quick thinking saved lives, but the damage was already done. As emergency teams arrived to tend to the injured, the reality of the situation became clear. The once-proud customer train had suffered a catastrophic derailment.

News of the accident spread quickly, and the public, who had once celebrated the customer train as a marvel of modern engineering, now demanded answers. Investigations revealed what many within the network had feared: the relentless pursuit of speed had compromised safety, and the warnings that had been ignored led directly to the derailment. The cracks in the tracks, which had gone unnoticed or unaddressed, were found to be the primary cause.

Aiden, the architect behind the efficiency push, faced the backlash with a mixture of denial and defiance. "We were doing what we thought was best for the future of the network," he insisted, even as the evidence mounted against him. But as more engineers, conductors, and maintenance workers came forward to speak about the pressures they had faced, it became clear that the problem was systemic. The pursuit of speed and profit had taken precedence over the very foundation of the customer train's mission.

Valen, who had tried to bridge the gap between tradition and progress, felt the weight of his choices. Standing before the press, he took responsibility for his role in allowing the shift to go unchecked. "We lost our way," he admitted. "We forgot that the customer train was not about speed or efficiency; it was about people, about the journey. And in our pursuit of progress, we abandoned our most important principles."

The derailment marked a turning point for the customer train network. In the aftermath, passengers who had once been loyal began to lose faith, choosing other means of travel. The stations, once symbols of community, became quiet as the number of passengers dwindled. The architects, engineers, and conductors who remained knew that they had reached a critical juncture—one that would determine the future of the customer train.

Amara, Suri, and Gregor, deeply affected by the tragedy, joined forces with Valen to begin the long process of rebuilding. They understood that restoring trust would not be easy, but they were committed to finding a way forward that honored both the lessons of the past and the potential of the future. They knew that the only way to move forward was to confront the mistakes of the present and return to the principles that had once made the customer train a symbol of hope and connection.

The derailment was a wake-up call, a reminder that speed without purpose is meaningless, and that efficiency without empathy leads only to disaster. As they began to plan for the restoration, they carried with them the knowledge that the journey ahead would be challenging, but also the hope that they could, once again, set the customer train back on the right track.

Part 3: The Restoration

Chapter VII: The Call for Change

In the wake of the derailment, the customer train network stood at a crossroads. The once-celebrated system now faced scrutiny from all sides. The stations, which had thrived with energy and community, became somber reminders of the tragedy. The trust and excitement that once defined the customer train had been replaced by hesitation and uncertainty. The architects knew that if they were to rebuild, they would need to do more than repair tracks—they would need to restore faith.

Valen, Amara, Suri, and Gregor gathered at **Platform Zero**, an old, abandoned station that had once served as the network's hub. It was a place of historical significance, where the original architects had first come together to lay the foundations of the customer train. The station's grandeur had faded over the years, but its symbolic power remained. The team chose this spot to begin their work—a place to reconnect with the past and chart a new course for the future.

Standing in the dusty, echoing halls of Platform Zero, Valen addressed the group. "We lost sight of our purpose," he began, his voice steady but filled with the weight of responsibility. "The derailment was the result of our own choices—choices driven by speed, efficiency, and profit. But now, we have a chance to change. We must find a way to restore the train's purpose and put passengers at the heart of our network again."

Suri, whose technology had become central to the automation of the system, nodded. "Technology is a powerful tool, but we misused it. We designed systems that replaced the human touch instead of enhancing it. We need to reimagine our technology, making it support the conductors and engineers so they can focus on the passengers and the experience, not just the performance metrics."

Amara, still in her conductor's uniform, looked out at the empty tracks. "We need to listen to our passengers again. They were our partners once, but we turned them into numbers on a screen. The customer train was always about connection. If we want to rebuild, we need to make passengers part of the journey once more."

The team knew that their path forward would not be easy. They had to confront the mistakes of the past and rebuild the train's infrastructure, not just in steel and technology, but in trust and relationships. They decided to launch a series of **Passenger Forums** at major stations, inviting passengers, conductors, engineers, and maintenance workers to come together and share their experiences. The forums would be places for open dialogue, where every voice would be heard and every suggestion considered.

The first forum took place at the newly reopened **Central Station**, once the crown jewel of the customer train network. Passengers arrived cautiously, uncertain of what to expect. But as they entered the station, they were greeted warmly by conductors and engineers, many of whom had been affected by the derailment themselves. The atmosphere was one of openness, a stark contrast to the efficiency-driven operations of recent years.

Lian, the young commuter who had felt the detachment growing within the network, attended the forum. She was surprised to see Valen, Amara, and Suri speaking directly with passengers, listening intently to their concerns. "This is what the customer train used to feel like," she thought, as she watched conductors guide conversations, making sure every voice was acknowledged. For the first time in years, she felt hope—a glimmer that the train she had loved as a child could return.

At the forum, Gregor shared insights into the state of the infrastructure and the plans for the future. "We are working to repair and strengthen the tracks," he explained. "But more importantly, we are committed to ensuring that safety and passenger comfort are our top priorities. We want every passenger to know that their journey is our responsibility."

Amara encouraged passengers to share their stories, and they spoke openly about their experiences. Some described the confusion and frustration they felt as the trains grew faster but less personal. Others shared memories of how conductors had once taken the time to connect with them, making their journeys feel special. One elderly passenger recalled how, years ago, she had met her husband aboard the customer train, and how the train had been a symbol of possibility and connection.

Valen took these stories to heart. "This is why we are here," he said, addressing the crowd. "We lost our way, but with your help, we can find it again. We want to build a network that not only gets you to your destination but makes you feel valued and connected along the way."

Suri, inspired by the conversations, committed herself to developing new systems that would use technology to enhance human interaction rather than replace it. She designed an interface that allowed passengers to communicate directly with conductors, engineers, and station personnel, ensuring that their needs and concerns were addressed in real-time. This technology also empowered conductors to take proactive steps, like adjusting routes based on passenger input or scheduling extra time for boarding when needed. The goal was clear: make technology the enabler of a better experience, not the barrier.

The forums continued, spreading to stations across the network. Each event brought new insights, and the team used the feedback to develop a new blueprint—a blueprint that blended the wisdom of the past with the advancements of the present. They began to restore the old stations, refurbishing them to feel warm and welcoming, while equipping them with technology that improved, rather than overshadowed, the passenger experience.

Valen, Gregor, Suri, and Amara worked closely with station managers and maintenance teams to prioritize the safety and integrity of the tracks. Engineers were retrained to focus not just on speed but on the quality of the ride. Conductors, once overwhelmed by efficiency targets, were given the freedom to engage with passengers, ensuring that every journey felt personal.

The response was overwhelming. Passengers who had once abandoned the customer train began returning, intrigued by the changes and excited to be part of the restoration. The atmosphere at stations became lively once again, with passengers sharing stories and conductors building connections that had been lost in the push for speed.

Lian watched the transformation with a sense of pride. She had seen the decline, but now she saw the restoration. She became a vocal advocate for the forums, helping conductors gather feedback and ensuring passengers felt included in the decision-making process. Her grandfather, who had spoken so fondly of the train's golden age, joined her at the stations, sharing his stories and encouraging others to believe in the train's revival.

As the forums gained momentum and the network adapted, the customer train began to find its way back. The new blueprint, born from the lessons of the past and the realities of the present, promised a future where the train could once again serve as a symbol of connection and progress.

The call for change had been answered, and the customer train, with its blend of tradition and innovation, set off on its journey of renewal. The tracks ahead were challenging, but the team knew that this time, they were moving in the right direction—one where technology and humanity traveled side by side.

Chapter VIII: The Architects of Renewal

The restoration of the customer train network had begun, but the work was far from complete. The forums and community outreach had rekindled trust and brought passengers back, but the architects knew that for the network to thrive sustainably, they needed to create a new blueprint—one that integrated the best of the past with the innovations of the present. This task fell to the team that had led the restoration efforts: Valen, Amara, Suri, Gregor, and now Lian, who had become a vocal advocate and leader among the new generation of passengers.

They met at **Platform of Renewal**, the newly restored station where the first forums had taken place. This time, the platform was buzzing with activity. Engineers, conductors, maintenance workers, and community leaders from various regions had gathered, eager to contribute to the new blueprint that would guide the future of the customer train. The team's vision was no longer just an idea; it was becoming a movement.

Valen opened the assembly, addressing the crowd that had gathered. "We have learned from our mistakes, and we have listened to the voices of our passengers. Today, we stand together to create a network that honors our original mission while embracing the innovations that can make every journey better. This is not just about rebuilding the customer train; it's about building a future we can all believe in."

The team presented their plan, which was based on three key pillars: **Connection, Adaptability, and Empowerment**. Each pillar was designed to ensure that the customer train remained relevant, sustainable, and, above all, centered on the needs of the passengers.

1. **Connection**: Amara spoke first, emphasizing the importance of building and maintaining personal connections within the network. "Our goal is to make every station a place where passengers feel welcome and valued," she explained. "We will reintroduce personal touch-points—conductors who know the regular passengers, station masters who offer assistance, and forums where everyone can share their experiences. Technology will support these efforts, but it will never replace them."

She detailed the new initiatives that would be implemented across the network. Conductors would be trained not just in logistics but in communication and empathy, ensuring that every interaction was meaningful. Stations would be equipped with digital kiosks designed to assist passengers without replacing the human staff, offering support where it was most needed.

1. **Adaptability**: Next, Gregor discussed the importance of creating a flexible and resilient infrastructure. "The customer train must be able to respond to the needs of the passengers and the communities it serves," he said. "Our new tracks will be designed for modular adaptation, allowing us to expand or change routes based on demand."

He explained the introduction of smaller, more agile trains that could operate on secondary routes, providing access to remote destinations and smaller communities. These trains would be supported by a dynamic scheduling system that could adjust in real-time, ensuring that no region was overlooked and that passengers had the freedom to travel as they wished.

1. **Empowerment**: Suri, whose technology had evolved to support the new vision, spoke next. "We are using technology not to replace people, but to empower them," she stated. "Our systems will provide conductors and engineers with the tools they need to make informed decisions, while passengers will have access to real-time information about their journeys, allowing them to engage more fully with the network."

She demonstrated a new interface that allowed passengers to communicate directly with conductors, request assistance, or provide feedback instantly. This interface, integrated into stations and mobile apps, ensured that passengers felt connected and heard at all times. The technology was designed to be transparent, showing how their feedback directly influenced schedules, routes, and services.

As the team outlined the new blueprint, the atmosphere in the room shifted from cautious optimism to excitement. The pillars of Connection, Adaptability, and Empowerment resonated with those who had seen the decline of the customer train and were eager for a new beginning. Lian, now standing among the team of architects, spoke on behalf of the passengers. "For years, we felt like we were just along for the ride, powerless to influence the journey. Today, that changes. This new blueprint gives us a voice and makes us partners in the journey."

Her words were met with applause, and the energy in the room was palpable. The architects, engineers, and conductors divided into groups, each tasked with developing specific projects that aligned with the new blueprint's pillars. They worked on designs for new passenger lounges that incorporated local art and culture, making stations feel like community hubs rather than transit points. They planned new training programs for staff that emphasized both technical skills and passenger engagement, ensuring that every employee felt empowered to contribute to the network's success.

Outside, as the team collaborated, trains continued to roll through the station, their rhythmic motion a reminder of the past and a promise of the future. The platform was alive again, filled with the sounds of collaboration and the hum of renewed purpose.

As the day concluded, Valen gathered the team for a final word. "We have laid the groundwork for a new era of the customer train. Our mission is clear: to create a network that connects, adapts, and empowers. It's up to us now to turn this vision into reality, to ensure that every passenger, every station, and every track serves its true purpose."

Suri smiled as she looked around at the people gathered. "This is what the customer train was always meant to be—a place where people come together, where technology supports humanity, and where every journey matters."

Amara, with her conductor's cap in hand, added, "We are not just restoring a train; we are restoring the spirit of the journey itself."

The architects of renewal knew they had taken the first step, but they also understood that the work ahead would require ongoing commitment, collaboration, and the courage to make difficult choices. Yet, for the first time in years, they felt hopeful. The new blueprint wasn't just about laying tracks—it was about laying the foundation for a future where technology and humanity traveled together, side by side.

And so, the customer train continued its journey. The tracks, restored and renewed, stretched out into the horizon, promising new adventures, destinations, and connections. The architects watched as the train pulled away, knowing that this was the beginning of something greater than any of them could have imagined—a future built on the strength of the past, the promise of the present, and the hope of what lay ahead.

Chapter IX: The New Blueprint

With the new blueprint finalized, the customer train network entered a phase of active transformation. The architects, engineers, conductors, and passengers worked together to implement the vision that had emerged from the forums and collaborative efforts. The new blueprint was more than a set of instructions—it was a living document that combined the wisdom of the past with the technological advancements of the present, ensuring that every decision was made with the passengers' experience in mind.

The implementation began at the newly designated **Hub of Renewal**, formerly Central Station, which was transformed into the heart of the network's revitalization efforts. The station, now a bustling hub of activity, served as a model for the entire system. It was outfitted with the latest technology to enhance passenger comfort while maintaining the station's historic charm, blending the old and the new seamlessly.

Lian stood at the entrance, watching as passengers streamed through. She felt a deep sense of pride as she saw the station come back to life. "This is what it should have always been—a place that feels like home, where every journey starts with purpose," she said to herself. Her role as a leader among the passenger community had grown, and she now worked closely with the architects, ensuring that every passenger's voice was heard in the ongoing transformation.

The new blueprint revolved around three main elements: **Personalized Journeys, Dynamic Infrastructure, and Integrated Technology**. Each element was designed to adapt and evolve, ensuring that the customer train could continue to meet the needs of its passengers, no matter how those needs changed.

1. **Personalized Journeys**: Amara, who had championed the importance of passenger connection, led the charge in redesigning the passenger experience. Conductors were trained to act as journey guides rather than mere operators, engaging with passengers from the moment they entered the station to the time they disembarked. "We are bringing the heart back into the customer train," she said during a training session with new conductors. "Our job is to know our passengers, understand their needs, and make every journey personal and memorable."

Stations were equipped with comfortable lounges that encouraged interaction among passengers, fostering a sense of community. Passengers could book specific carriages tailored to their needs—quiet cars for those seeking solitude, collaborative spaces for business travelers, and family-friendly cars with amenities for children. The goal was to create an experience that went beyond transportation, turning each journey into an opportunity for connection and growth.

1. **Dynamic Infrastructure**: Gregor's team focused on building a flexible and resilient track system that could adapt to changes in passenger demand. "The future of the customer train lies in our ability to respond quickly and effectively," he explained during a meeting with engineers. "We are designing tracks that can shift and adjust, allowing us to create new routes as needed and to maintain service even during challenging conditions."

The new tracks were supported by modular technology, allowing sections to be upgraded or rerouted with minimal disruption. This system not only improved safety but also gave the customer train the ability to expand into new regions quickly, bringing access to communities that had previously been disconnected. Gregor's team also prioritized environmental sustainability, using eco-friendly materials and renewable energy sources to power the trains and stations.

1. **Integrated Technology**: Suri's vision for technology integration became the backbone of the network's evolution. She developed a comprehensive digital platform that connected every aspect of the journey—from the moment a passenger purchased a ticket to their interaction with conductors and station staff. "Technology should support the journey, not overshadow it," she explained with her faithful mantra at a technology summit. "Our systems will

empower conductors, provide passengers with seamless access to information, and ensure that we remain adaptable in a rapidly changing world."

The platform allowed passengers to personalize their experience, offering real-time updates on train schedules, routes, and conditions. It also gave passengers the ability to provide feedback directly to conductors and engineers, ensuring that their voices influenced decisions in real-time. The technology was designed to be intuitive and user-friendly, with a focus on enhancing—not replacing—the human element.

The changes began to take hold, and the results were immediate. Passengers who had once felt like numbers on a schedule now felt recognized and valued. Conductors, empowered with the freedom to engage with passengers, rekindled the spirit of connection that had once defined the customer train. Engineers, supported by advanced diagnostic tools and dynamic track systems, worked with a renewed sense of purpose, knowing that their efforts were directly impacting the quality of each journey.

The stations, once impersonal transit hubs, were alive with activity. At the Hub of Renewal, musicians played during peak hours, local artisans sold their crafts, and food vendors offered cuisine that reflected the culture of the region. The station had become a destination in itself—a place where passengers lingered, shared stories, and became part of a larger community. The architects' vision of a customer train network that not only transported people but connected lives was becoming a reality.

Valen, observing the transformation, felt a renewed sense of pride. "This is the blueprint we needed," he said to his colleagues during a meeting at the Hub. "It's not just about building tracks or designing schedules; it's about creating a system that evolves with our passengers and adapts to their needs."

The new blueprint's impact was most visible during the launch of the **Adaptive Route Initiative**. This program allowed smaller trains to respond dynamically to passenger demand, creating new routes on short notice and ensuring that even the most remote stations received service. Valen, Amara, Gregor, and Suri joined the inaugural journey of one such train, which traveled to a small village that had long been isolated from the main network.

As the train pulled into the village station, they were greeted by the community—children waving, local leaders expressing their gratitude, and passengers stepping off the train with a sense of excitement. The architects had not only restored the customer train; they had expanded its reach, bringing new opportunities and connections to places that had once been overlooked.

Lian, who had helped design the route, watched with satisfaction. "This is the power of the customer train," she said. "It's not about the destination alone; it's about the journey and the people we meet along the way."

The customer train, once at risk of losing its soul, had found its way back. The blueprint ensured that the network could continue to grow and evolve while staying true to its purpose. Technology, infrastructure, and human connection worked together seamlessly, creating a system that could withstand the challenges of the future while honoring the legacy of its past.

As the architects, engineers, conductors, and passengers celebrated the success of the new blueprint, the train pulled away from the village, its whistle echoing through the hills. The tracks ahead were clear, and the journey continued—one filled with promise, connection, and the knowledge that every destination was a shared achievement.

The customer train, reborn through the efforts of those who believed in its potential, moved forward, carrying not only passengers but the hope of a network that had learned from its past and embraced its future.

10

Epilogue: The Tracks Ahead

Years had passed since the restoration of the customer train network, and its transformation had become a benchmark for progress and balance. The Hub of Renewal, once a symbol of decline, was now a vibrant epicenter where passengers, conductors, and engineers mingled freely, sharing stories and experiences. The customer train had become more than a mode of transportation; it was a thriving community on wheels, connecting people across cities, countries, and continents.

The new blueprint—crafted from the wisdom of the original architects and enhanced by modern technology—continued to evolve. Each station, now a hub of local culture and connection, reflected the spirit of its community, ensuring that passengers felt at home no matter where their journey took them. The forums that had been central to the restoration efforts became a permanent fixture, giving passengers a voice and making them active participants in the future of the network.

Valen, now a senior advisor to the network, walked through the Hub of Renewal, observing the lively atmosphere. Families gathered in the lounges, travelers exchanged ideas, and conductors moved with purpose, greeting passengers with the warmth that had once defined the golden age of the customer train. "This is what we envisioned," he said, a sense of fulfillment in his voice. "We've created something that belongs to everyone."

Amara, who had taken on a leadership role overseeing conductor training, joined him. "It's more than a train now; it's a movement," she said. "We've built a system where passengers are more than just customers—they're partners. Every day, we see people building connections, finding opportunities, and creating memories."

Suri, whose technological innovations had played a pivotal role in the network's rebirth, was now focused on future-proofing the system. "Technology continues to evolve, but we've learned that its greatest power is its ability to enhance human connection, not replace it," she explained at one of the network's technology summits. "We'll keep innovating, but always with the understanding that our goal is to empower people, not automate their experiences away."

Gregor, who had become a mentor to the next generation of engineers, stood at the controls of one of the newly designed engines. His years of experience had taught him the importance of adaptability, and he worked tirelessly to ensure that every track and every train met the highest standards of safety and reliability. "The future is about resilience," he said during a training session. "We build tracks that last, and we create routes that respond to the changing needs of our passengers."

Lian, who had grown from a passenger advocate into a prominent voice in the network's leadership, spoke at the launch of a new community initiative. "The customer train is not just about reaching destinations quickly; it's about making sure the journey is meaningful," she declared. "We have the ability to shape how people connect, how communities thrive, and how we all move forward together."

The passenger forums, which continued to expand to every corner of the network, had become the backbone of the customer train's success. Each forum served as a platform for passengers, conductors, engineers, and station staff to share their ideas and concerns. From these forums emerged new routes, improved services, and innovations that kept the network aligned with the needs of its passengers. The dynamic, evolving nature of the forums ensured that the customer train remained relevant, adaptable, and deeply connected to its communities.

The Adaptive Route Initiative, which had begun as a pilot project, became one of the network's most celebrated achievements. By responding to the real-time needs of passengers, the customer train extended its reach into remote and underserved regions, fostering economic growth and cultural exchange. Valen and his team often traveled on these new routes, witnessing firsthand the impact of their work. They saw how the train, once a symbol of technology and speed alone, had become a beacon of opportunity and connection.

The architects who had led the renewal effort were now celebrated as visionaries. Their efforts were chronicled not just as a story of restoration but as a blueprint for anyone seeking to balance innovation with human values. The customer train's transformation became a beacon for all people and cultures, demonstrating that progress and empathy could coexist when purpose guided every decision.

The train, still a gleaming engineering marvel, continued to move forward. Its strengthened and expanded tracks carried passengers to wonderous destinations. The sound of the train's whistle echoed across valleys and cities, a reminder that the journey was more than just about speed; it was about the people and places it connected.

As the sun dipped below the horizon, casting a golden glow over the tracks, the architects gathered at the Hub of Renewal to reflect on their journey. They knew that their work was ongoing, that the customer train would need to keep evolving to meet the challenges of the future. But they also knew that as long as they remained committed to their principles—connection, adaptability, and empowerment—the customer train would continue to thrive.

Valen raised a toast with his colleagues, their glasses clinking in the soft evening light. "To the customer train," he said, "and to every journey yet to come."

The customer train moved steadily into the night, its brightness a lighthouse in the distance. For all those on board, and all those yet to join, the promise of connection, progress, and a shared future awaited. The tracks ahead were long, but they were guided by the vision of a network that had learned from its past, embraced its present, and looked forward to its future with hope.